Be My Friend

Grade 1

UNIT 2 BOOK 1

Program Authors

Carl Bereiter, Ph.D.
Andrew Biemiller, Ph.D.
Joe Campione, Ph.D.
Doug Fuchs, Ph.D.
Lynn Fuchs, Ph.D.

Steve Graham, Ph.D.
Karen Harris, Ph.D.
Jan Hirshberg, Ed.D.
Anne McKeough, Ph.D.
Marsha Roit, Ed.D.

Marlene Scardamalia, Ph.D.
Marcy Stein, Ph.D.
Gerald H. Treadway Jr, Ph.D.

Photo Credits

4 tuja66/iStock/Getty Images Plus; **5** Jupiterimages/Getty Images, Floresco Productions/Cultura/Getty Images, NewStock/Alamy; **52** Image Source/Corbis. **Back Cover:** Jupiterimages/Getty Images, Floresco Productions/Cultura/Getty Images, NewStock/Alamy.

Acknowledgment

Grateful acknowledgment is given to the following publishers and copyright owners for permissions granted to reprint selections from their publications. All possible care has been taken to trace ownership and secure permission for each selection included. In case of any errors or omissions, the Publisher will be pleased to make suitable acknowledgments in future editions.

Chicken Chickens Go to School by Valeri Gorbachev. Copyright ©2003 by Valeri Gorbachev. All rights reserved. Used by permission from North-South Books Inc., New York.

MHEonline.com

Copyright © 2016 McGraw-Hill Education

All rights reserved. No part of this publication may be reproduced or distributed in any form or by any means, or stored in a database or retrieval system, without the prior written consent of McGraw-Hill Education, including, but not limited to, network storage or transmission, or broadcast for distance learning.

Send all inquiries to:
McGraw-Hill Education
8787 Orion Place
Columbus, OH 43240

ISBN: 978-0-07-667456-5
MHID: 0-07-667456-8

Printed in the United States of America.

7 8 9 MER 25 24 23

UNIT 2 Be My Friend

Book 1

Table of Contents

Unit Overview 4

Chicken Chickens Go to School 6
    written and illustrated by Valeri Gorbachev

A Friend Can 32
    by Harper Hess
    illustrated by Janet McDonnell

My Two Best Friends 34
    by Claire Daniel
    illustrated by Mark Rogalski

Glossary 52

UNIT 2 | Be My Friend

Theme Connections

How are these children being good friends?

Background Builder Video
connected.mcgraw-hill.com

Essential Question How do you make new friends?

Chicken Chickens Go to School

by Valeri Gorbachev

One fine day, Mother Hen took her two little chickens to school for the very first time.

The little chickens were a little scared.

"Don't worry," said Mother Hen as she waved good-bye, "I'm sure you will like it here."

"Hello," said Mrs. Heron the teacher, "welcome to my class."

"We're scared," said the chickens. "We don't know anyone."

"Don't worry," said Mrs. Heron. "I'm sure you will make friends quickly."

"Can we make friends with anyone in the class?" asked the chickens.

Mrs. Heron smiled. "Of course you can," she said.

During playtime, all the chickens could think about was making friends.

Beaver is very big, they thought. It would be good to have her as a friend. So they walked up to Beaver and said hello.

"Sssssssssh," said Beaver, "I'm trying to build this tower!"

During story time, the chickens sat next to Rabbit. Rabbit looks friendly, they thought. He would be a good friend. So they turned to Rabbit and said hello.

"Sssssssssh," said Rabbit, "I'm listening to the story."

During music time the chickens stood next to Frog. Frog is little just like us, thought the chickens. Maybe he would be our friend. So the chickens turned to Frog and said hello.

"Sssssssssh," said Frog, "I'm trying to sing."

During snack time the two little chickens sat all by themselves. No one wants to make friends with us, they thought.

"How do you like school?" asked Mrs. Heron.

"We can't make any friends," said the little chickens sadly.

"Just wait," said Mrs. Heron. "I have a feeling you will."

After everyone cleaned up, it was time to go outside.

"Come along," said Mrs. Heron. "We'll go to the meadow."

The whole class cheered.

On the way, everyone crossed a little stream. Everyone except the little chickens.

"What's wrong?" asked Mrs. Heron.

"We're too little," said the chickens. "We might fall off the rocks—and we can't swim!"

"Don't be such chicken chickens," said Beaver. "The water isn't very deep. You can do it."

"No," they said. "We're just little chickens."

"I could build a bridge over the water," said Beaver.

"I could leap across the stream carrying the chickens," said Rabbit.

"I could teach the chickens how to swim," said Frog.

"Thank you all," said Mrs. Heron, "but I have a better idea. Why don't you hold hands with the chickens and help them over the rocks?"

So they all held hands and slowly crossed the stream.

"We did it!" cried the little chickens.
"Thank you for helping us."

The little chickens had a wonderful time playing in the meadow with their new friends.

On the way back to school, the little chickens scampered across the rocks all by themselves.

"Hurray for the little chickens!" everyone cried.

After school Mother Hen was waiting. "Goodness," she said as the little chickens ran down the stairs. "You both look very happy."

"We *like* school," they said. "We made lots of friends."

"That's wonderful," said Mother Hen.

As the little chickens headed home they turned and waved.

"Good-bye, friends," they called, "see you tomorrow!"

When I need help, who can help me?
A friend can help me.

When I want to play, who can play with me?
A friend can play with me.

When I am laughing, who can laugh with me?
A friend can laugh with me.

When I am sad, who can cheer me up?
A friend can cheer me up.

When I am angry, who can comfort me?
A friend can comfort me.

When I have done something wrong,
who can forgive me?
A friend can forgive me.

Essential Question How can you be a good friend to more than one person at a time?

My Two Best Friends

by Claire Daniel
illustrated by Mark Rogalski

I have a best friend problem. I don't have one best friend. I have two!

Carlos is my oldest friend. He is good at sports. He likes to play games, like kickball. Carlos taught me how to kick the ball really far.

Sometimes he says, "You are my best friend, Trung."

I don't know what to say when he says that. I like Carlos a lot, but I have another best friend too.

Hal is my other best friend. He and I play together a lot. Sometimes we play computer games. Sometimes we paint pictures, or we might take a walk. We enjoy each other's company.

Sometimes Hal says, "Who is your best friend, Trung? Is it me?"

I don't know what to say. Hal is my best friend, but so is Carlos.

Carlos, Hal, and I play together at recess. Most days we play kickball, but today was different.

Carlos said, "Come on, let's go! Let's choose teams!"

Hal hung back.

"What's wrong?" I asked.

"I don't want to play kickball," he replied.

"Why not?" Carlos asked.

"I always get chosen last," Hal said. "I can't kick well."

"Ah, come on, don't be stubborn!" Carlos said.

"No," Hal said. "I'm not going."

He crossed his arms across his chest.

Hal glanced at me. "If you are my friend, then you won't go either," he said. "Let's go play on the playground."

Carlos replied, "Hold on! Trung is *my* best friend. He is playing kickball with me." Carlos tugged on my arm.

Hal looked at me. "I thought *I* was your best friend," he said.

"Hal, you *are* my best friend," I replied. Then I turned to Carlos. "And *you* are my best friend too," I said.

"You can only have one best friend!" Carlos insisted.

"That's right," Hal said.

"So you have to choose," Carlos said.

"I disagree," I replied. "I think you can have more than one best friend."

A boy threw the ball toward us. Carlos caught it.

"So make a decision already!" Hal said. I just stood there, because I did not want to choose. Carlos started walking toward the group of kids playing kickball.

Hal looked at his feet. He did not say a word.

"Wait!" I said.

Carlos turned around. Hal looked up. Both boys looked at me.

"Why can't all three of us be best friends?" I asked.

"I have an idea," I said. "Carlos, remember when you taught me how to kick the ball? Why don't you teach Hal how to kick too? Then he will enjoy the game more, and we can all play together. What do you think, Hal?"

"Maybe," Hal said, "but what about Carlos? He does not want to go to the playground."

"Why don't we take turns?" I asked. "Today we can do one thing. Tomorrow we can do something else."

Carlos put the ball on the ground. Then he showed Hal how to kick it.

"Here, try it," Carlos said. "Tomorrow we can play a game on the playground."

And I smiled because that's what best friends do.

Glossary

B

better
more useful or improved

C

chicken
someone who is afraid

company
being with another person

cried
a form of the verb **cry**: to shout with emotion

E

except
not including (someone or something)

F

feeling
a sense of something

fine
very good

G

glanced
a form of the verb **glance**: to look at something quickly

J

just
exactly

S

scampered
a form of the verb **scamper**: to run or move quickly, often in a playful way